Daring to Follow Jesus

Stephen D. & Jacalyn Eyre

A Month
of
Guided
Quiet
Times

INTERVARSITY PRESS
DOWNERS GROVE, ILLINOIS 60515

InterVarsity Press® is the book-publishing division of InterVarsity Christian Fellowship®, a student movement active on campus at hundreds of universities, colleges and schools of nursing in the United States of America, and a member movement of the International Fellowship of Evangelical Students. For information about local and regional activities, write Public Relations Dept., InterVarsity Christian Fellowship, 6400 Schroeder Rd., P.O. Box 7895, Madison, WI 53707-7895.

Cover photograph: Tim Nyberg

ISBN 0-8308-1179-6

Printed in the United States of America ∞

15	14	13	12	11	10	9	8	7	6	5	4	3	2	1
03	02	01	00	99	98	97	96	95	94	93				

Introducing Daring to Follow Jesus

Worshiping God is revolutionary. It threatens the established powers and patterns of life.

When Moses approached Pharaoh to let Israel go from their bondage and slavery, he asked that Israel be allowed to go into the desert for three days to worship God. Pharaoh was not pleased and the battle began. That request for freedom to worship began the process that led to the exodus and Israel's deliverance from slavery.

Make no mistake, in a fallen world the worship of God is an act of insurrection. As we worship, we lift our eyes beyond the here and now to the eternal. We lift our hearts from the mud of mixed motives to the unadulterated good. We look past the dark god of this age to the God of eternal light.

If you set your heart to worship Jesus Christ, you won't have to deal with Pharaoh, but you will encounter massive forces of opposition. From your responsibilities you will encounter resistance. From your most important relationships you will encounter resistance. From outside and inside your soul you will encounter resistance.

Of the variety of forces that we all encounter in the worship of God, two of the most dangerous and powerful are so entrenched in our culture that you probably don't even see them or know how they affect you.

Civil Religion

In the fourth century the Roman emperor Constantine saw a cross in the sky before a major battle and heard the words "By this sign, conquer." After his victory, in gratitude for the perceived divine aid, he made Christianity the official religion of the Roman Empire. That was the beginning of Christendom. While it may have made being a Christian immeasurably less dangerous, it made following Jesus Christ immeasurably more difficult.

The problems created by Constantinism come from a merging of the State and the church. The result of the wedding was that it created a civil religion with God as the official deity. This may sound like a good move, but God's presence was lost in the institutional structures of society. Just as a person became a citizen of the State at birth, one also automatically became a member of the church. Instead of personal conversion and a life of faith, knowing God was merely a matter of obeying the laws of the government and following the religious requirements of the church.

Secular Society

Modernity is a way of thinking that grew out of the Enlightenment in the eighteenth century. Modernity, among other things, was a reaction to Constantinism. Feeling oppressed by the vast institutional structures of a thousand years of Christendom, the framers of the modern age sought to build a secular society. The goal was to escape from the monolithic presence of the church and at the same time create new forms of democratic government, thus liberating society from the entrenched rule of "divine-right" elites comprised of the royal families of Europe.

In the process of creating the modern world, God was culturally exiled. Education and research were conducted without reference to God's revelation. Personal fulfillment was sought now without a sense of membership in God's people. Rules for morality were conceived without a concern for God's will.

A Dying Legacy

Constantinism has been dying a slow death for a couple of hundred years under the barrage of modernism. Likewise, modernity is dying a slow death. It is now revealing its spiritual and moral bankruptcy on the streets of our cities, in the epidemic of suicides among our youth and by the international collapse of Marxism.

As these powers pass away, they have both left us with a devastating spiritual legacy—the sense of God's absence. Constantinism obscures God by making him synonymous with the cultural structures. He vanishes in cultural immanence. Modernity obscures God by exiling him to the borders of our cultural institutions and mental consciousness. Who expects to meet him in the day-to-day issues and activities of life?

A Revolutionary Vision

It is possible to worship God and fellowship with him in the day-to-day issues of life. He is here in his world. He has promised to be with his people. The heavens declare his glory. The challenge for Christians is that we must learn how to meet with him and then determine to do it. We believe that it is possible to penetrate the barriers created by Constantinism and modernity by the practice of a personal quiet time and the use of spiritual disciplines. It is to this end that we write the Spiritual Encounter Guides.

Daring to Follow Jesus grows out of our experience of Christian ministry on both sides of the Atlantic. During our time in England, it seemed to us that there was a great deal more emphasis on the cross of Christ than we heard in the American church. In fellowship with our British friends, we learned deeper ways in which the work of Jesus on the cross opens up the riches of God's grace. On the other hand, our experience in the American church was on the lordship of Jesus Christ. Jesus is Lord

over every area of life, thinking, working, family, politics and it is the
Christian's responsibility to work this out day-by-day and moment-by-
moment.

Having tasted the benefits of both emphases, we wanted to bring them
together in a guide that looks long and hard at the cross of Christ for the
day-to-day issues of Christian living, not just for conversion. Likewise,
we wanted to write in a way that applies the lordship of Christ to every
facet of life in a culture that seeks to confine his influence to an hour or
two on Sunday morning.

The Shape of the Guide

You will spend six days in each of the four Gospels and six days in the
Epistles. As the different-colored panes of glass in a stained-glass window of a church combine to give a picture, so the Gospels and epistles
give a different color and piece of the picture of the ministry of Jesus.
Each piece of the picture may be worth looking at individually, but you
don't get the total picture unless you put them all together.

Starting in *Mark*, you will look at the beginnings of Jesus' ministry as
he called the disciples. You will taste Mark's style of focusing on the
actions of Jesus.

In *Matthew* you will study at what Jesus taught the disciples about
how to live life in his kingdom. You will get a glimpse of Matthew's
concern that we see Jesus as the King and Lawgiver of the new Israel.

In *Luke* you will learn of the saving purpose of Jesus' ministry as he
goes to Jerusalem to be crucified. You will gain insight into Luke's
understanding of Jesus' secret ambition to die for us.

In *John* you will study and pray through Jesus' death on the cross and
the events surrounding his resurrection. You will see that John wrote so
that those who read would believe.

In the *Epistles* you will see what the lordship of Christ and the cross
of Christ means for Christians as we live waiting for Jesus' return.

Writing this guide was a team effort. In the introductions you'll read stories from Steve's experience, and in the study sections you'll see more of Jackie's hand.

Using the Guide

Some people think of a quiet time as being Bible study and prayer. We think of a quiet time as an opportunity to meet with God—in which you do Bible study and pray. The difference between the two definitions, may seem small, but we think it is crucial. If a quiet time is just Bible study and prayer, then the relational dimension may easily get lost. You may end up merely going through the motions of religious activities and gaining some new information. However, if your goal is to set aside time to meet with God, then the whole dynamic of the quiet time is changed. It becomes a cultivation of a relationship and an opportunity for discipleship as the Lord meets with us.

Of course, because God's Word is his means of instructing us, we can't expect to learn from him unless we are spending serious time considering what has been written down for us. Likewise, prayer is the means by which we talk with him and ask for his help. But we must make sure that our prayer involves listening as well as asking. If we allow our prayer to degenerate into offering God a list of our desires and our recommendations for running the world, then we are no longer in a personal teacher-student relationship.

The format for each day in *Daring to Follow Jesus,* as with all Spiritual Encounter Guides includes five elements:

Introduction: This allows us to set the tone and introduce the day's issues for your quiet time.

Approach: This section is designed to help you to deal with mental and emotional obstacles that we all struggle with as we seek to shift our attention from ourselves to pay attention to God and his word. Take some time with the approach question—five minutes or more. Use it to reach out to God so that you know you are meeting with him as you begin your study of his Word.

Study: These questions are written to help you focus on the content of the passage. They focus on the essential issues of each passage and on what they mean.

Reflect: In this section, we use the spiritual tools of silence and imagination to help you apply the passage to your soul and life issues. Like the approach question, the more time you take with these questions, the more you will come away from your quiet time with a sense of personal encounter.

Pray: We offer a couple of suggestions for prayer. We expect during this time that you will develop your own prayer list as well. Take time to ask God for help and wisdom for yourself, your family, church, friends and whatever else you can think of. If you don't have a prayer list, you may find the chart at the back of the guide helpful.

Approach	Study
Reflect	Pray

How to Think About Quiet Time

A word of caution: this guide is not intended to make you feel guilty. It's a funny thing, but in our experience, people who don't have quiet times don't feel much guilt about it. On the other hand, people who think that quiet times are important often experience a good deal of guilt. It seems that the expectation on the part of many people is that you must have one every day or else you will be a spiritual failure. Quiet time guides can nourish this inclination because it is obvious when it has been a couple days since you last used the guide. Of course, this guilt feeds on itself and after awhile you avoid the guide altogether because you don't want to confront your sense of failure.

We like the advice that Brother Lawrence gave in *The Practice of the Presence of God.* He wrote that he never condemned himself for missing the mark in his times with God. He knew that God was not surprised at his "failure"; instead, he knew that God was delighted whenever he took time to pray. After all, God is not a petulant father who scolds us when we don't write home. If you follow his example, you will discover that you will choose to meet with God, not because you have to, but because you desire to.

In order to keep this guide from being a "guilt producer" we have not divided it by weeks. Instead, we have merely numbered the days. Some weeks you may have a quiet time six out of seven days. That's great! Other weeks you may have only one or two. That's still great! God doesn't love you more on the weeks that you have a quiet time every day or less on the weeks when you have no quiet time at all. God loves you through the free grace given to you by faith in Jesus Christ.

Daring to follow Jesus is a challenge, a difficult one. Many have attempted it and fallen back along the way. However, many have been faithful all the way through this world and on into the next. We write this guide to share with you in the adventure of discipleship.

"Come, follow me," Jesus said, "and I will make you fishers of men" (Matthew 4:20).

"If anyone would come after me, he must deny himself and take up his cross and follow me. For whoever wants to save his life will lose it, but whoever loses his life for me will find it" (Matthew 16:24).

"Jesus said to them, 'I tell you the truth, . . . every one who has left house or brothers or sisters or father or mother or children or fields for my sake will receive a hundred times as much and will inherit eternal life. But many who are first will be last, and many who are last will be first' " (Matthew 19:28-20).

Following Jesus is revolutionary for those who are willing to take the risk.

DAY 1

The Beginning of the Gospel
Mark 1:1-8

---

*N*ew things are exciting. "Bigger," "better," "newer" are the words the advertisers use to get us to sit up and pay attention to their products. New cars shine, smell fresh and drive with zip. New clothes look sharp and keep us in style. The problem with new things, however, is that they get old. Today's new clothes will be out of style next year. And besides that, they stop holding their shape and begin to look shabby. New cars lose their shine, get dents and upkeep costs increase to the point that we eventually want to get rid of them.

But what if there was something that was always new, fresh and just beginning that never got old? What if the excitement of new ideas and fresh opportunities kept on forever?

That is what the gospel of Jesus Christ is like. It began 2,000 years ago with the ministry of John the Baptist and Jesus, but, because it is about the eternal God who is the source of new life, it never gets old.

When we read about the events of the gospel in the New Testament, we are never reading about things that just happened long ago and ended. What we are reading about is the start-up of the ministry of Jesus which began then and, because he rose from the dead, will continue on forever. This means that you and I can get in on the action. We too can be a part of this world-changing, life-changing good news ministry of Jesus Christ.

The six quiet times in the Gospel of Mark are written so that you can read about what Jesus did and is still doing so that you too can enter into those events yourself.

Approach
When you enter a movie theater, your sense of enjoyment is enhanced because you are in a dark room with no windows and therefore outside distractions are cut off. In addition, the screen you view is large, and you are surrounded with sound. Your sense of encounter with the Lord will be enhanced if you put yourself physically and emotionally in a place where you can be alone with the Lord. Seek to focus on God and write down every distraction that comes your way for the next five or ten minutes.

After you have written down your distractions ask him to prepare you and empower you spiritually to enter into the Gospel of Mark. Write out your prayer.

Study

1. Read Mark 1:1-8. In verse 1, Mark writes about the beginning of the gospel. Describe what is going on in these verses, noting such things as the people, places and times mentioned.

2. There is a great sense of anticipation as the people come to hear John. In your own words, what is John's message (vv. 7-8)?

3. What is the difference between John and the coming One?

4. The people are coming out from Jerusalem to seek a solution for their sins. We don't use the term *sin* much in our culture anymore. What is sin?

How does a sense of sinfulness affect people?

Reflect

1. Place yourself in this crowd gathering to hear John's message. What feelings do you have?

2. John called people to turn away from their sins in order to get ready for the coming of the Messiah. What things do you need to turn away from in order to grow in the knowledge of Jesus Christ?

3. Some people think verse one is the title for the whole book of Mark, not just the opening verses. Read it again, and write out what it says in your own words.

If the gospel began in Mark and is still continuing, that means you and I can participate in it! How would you like to experience the spiritual truth of these verses in your life now?

Pray
Pray for our world, that the message of Jesus Christ would bring a turning from sinfulness to the forgiveness that he offers.

Pray that the church would continually prepare itself to welcome Jesus.

DAY 2

Introducing Jesus
Mark 1:9-13

I never really expected to meet Jesus Christ.

As a kid he seemed to me to be some guy in white robes coming in from the clouds as he was beautifully portrayed on the huge stained-glass window at the back of our church. We sang about him, we heard sermons about him, but he wasn't someone that I could personally know. First of all, he lived a long time ago. Second, he was supposed to have gone to heaven. Either way he wasn't anywhere that I could encounter him.

But then I met a few people who were convinced that they knew him personally and that I could too. My first response was to write them off as mentally unstable. Religious fanatics, you know. The problem was, they were so abnormal in the best kind of way. I liked them, something about them rang true.

After a while I began to listen to what they had to say about Jesus. It was because of these people that I was ready when the spiritual knock came to me. One day I opened the door to find that somebody by the name of Jesus, someone I couldn't see but was there nevertheless, inviting me into a personal relationship with him.

Since the beginning, God has called people to meet his Son. Initially, he sent John the Baptist to get people ready. Then he followed up with a few good words of his own. He often does the same thing today sending people to prepare us (like a friend or minister) and then personally calling on us.

Approach

Jesus Christ wants to have a personal encounter with you. Imagine there is a door on your heart. Listen for the knocking of the Lord. Open it up and invite him in. Write down what it's like to be in the presence of the living Lord.

Study

1. Read Mark 1:9-13. List the events that take place.

2. What would have been seen and heard at Jesus' baptism?

How is the entire Trinity involved?

3. Jesus' choice of baptism as the means to begin his public ministry is striking. What motive could Jesus have for seeking baptism if he was the pleasing Son of God who didn't need to be forgiven?

4. When Jesus was in the desert, separated from people, he was tempted by Satan and attended by angels. How do you think this challenging experience of forty days of fasting, temptation and divine provision in the desert helped prepare Jesus for his ministry?

Reflect
1. The Father proclaims he is well pleased with Jesus. As you begin this study of discipleship, write down some of the things you feel about Jesus.

2. At this point in Jesus' life, he needed to hear God affirm his identity. What do you need to hear from God for the issues that you face?

3. As the voice spoke, heaven was "torn open." What are the barriers that need to be torn open between you and God?

Pray
Pray for your friends at school, in your work and in your neighborhood. Ask God to give them a hunger to learn about Jesus Christ.

DAY 3
The Call of Jesus
Mark 1:14-20

Recently I went to an Elton John concert. It's a good thing that I went to *hear* him, because I certainly didn't see very much of him. Our seats were on the grass at the back of the crowd, and he appeared to be a small figure, about an inch high, way down on the stage. Although I did get to look through someone's field glasses, even then I couldn't see his face—but I did see him change his orange coat for a purple one.

In some ways that is how I used to think about Jesus and Christianity. I envisioned myself coming in the back door of a huge auditorium filled with people. Way at the front was this figure that I could hardly see. I felt sure that he never saw me come in, didn't know my name and wouldn't notice when I left.

However, I couldn't have been more wrong. Every person that enters his church comes in by means of a personal invitation. Just as he called the first disciples, so he continues to do so throughout the years.

The way he extends his call varies. Some hear his call through a friend, some hear his call through a preacher or evangelist, some hear his call through reading the Bible, and some in the midst of some mundane activity feel a pull on their hearts. But however it comes, Jesus Christ by the Spirit says to every believer, "Come, follow me, and I will make you fishers of men."

Approach
The Lord has his ways of getting our attention despite our preoccupations and busyness. But when we stop to listen, we open up to new depths of discipleship. Sit quietly for a couple minutes, then make a list of things that keep your attention and could get in the way of hearing the Lord's constant call on your life.

Study
1. Read Mark 1:14-20. Look at verse 15. Write out in your own words Jesus' message of the good news of God.

What is good about it?

2. What does Jesus require of the disciples he calls?

3. How do you think the families of the new disciples might have felt about Jesus?

4. If these verses were the only description of Jesus you had, how would you describe his style and priorities?

Reflect

1. Discipleship begins with Jesus' call. In what ways have you sensed the call of Jesus?

2. Discipleship to Jesus requires a turning away from your own agenda to his. Consider the patterns of your life. Do you live now by your own agenda or his? Give specific examples.

3. Reflect on how Jesus' call impacts how you should think about the world. Sit quietly in a prayerful attitude, and make a list of the major relationships and responsibilities in your life. Lay each one before Jesus, and ask him how he wants you to think, feel and act about each one.

Pray

Pray that the members of your church would make obedience to Jesus the number-one priority in their lives.

Pray that the members of God's church would be faithful fishers of humanity, inviting others to hear the good news.

DAY 4
Power over Evil
Mark 1:21-28

*A*s a boy I was afraid to put my hand over the side of the bed. I was sure that something underneath would pull me under. Then there were those times I had to get up in the middle of the night to go to the bathroom. Walking down a dark hallway, I found the strength to take on the dark passageway by reciting part of the Twenty-third Psalm that I had learned in Sunday school, "Even though I walk through the valley of the shadow of death, I will fear no evil, for you are with me; your rod and your staff, they comfort me."

I am tempted to laugh at those childish fears now but I don't. My fears, which were no different from those of my own children or of those around the world, reflect a sense of danger in the world. Something somewhere is not right. The world is not a completely safe place.

We see the effects of evil on the news: war, murder, robbery, rape. And we see some people being "brought to justice." But even if it were possible to round up every criminal in the country and put them in prison, we still would not feel safe, or *be* safe. There is an Evil One, a spiritual being that fuels the ills and pains of this world. As one songwriter put it, "The enemy is bigger than the one who pulls the trigger."

We don't talk much about demons, Satan or evil today. Frequently, they are dismissed as superstitions. However, those who follow Jesus Christ should know better. He is able to unmask evil. Those who dismiss the evil in the world will never know their true need for Jesus.

Approach

One of David's favorite ways to describe God in the Psalms is to picture him as a fortress. In order to help you settle in God's presence, write out all the pressures that you face and which you feel threatening you. Then imagine that you are safely surrounded by God as a fortress. Write down how you feel.

Study

1. Read Mark 1:21-28. The synagogue was where the Jewish people gathered weekly to worship. What would be the strategic benefit for Jesus of beginning his ministry in the synagogue?

2. What might Jesus' encounter with the demon in the synagogue imply about the spiritual condition of Israel?

3. Describe the confrontation between Jesus and the evil spirit.

4. Jesus' display of authority impressed the people. Where else have you seen the authority of Jesus displayed in the preceding verses (1:12-20)?

Reflect

1. To appreciate what happened in the synagogue between Jesus and the demon we need to acknowledge the presence and power of evil in the world. In what ways do you see evil at work in your life?

in the church?

in your nation?

in the world?

2. Close your eyes and meditate on Jesus' victory over evil. Write down an area that you listed in reflection question one.

Picture Jesus coming face to face with it and bringing it under his authority. How do you respond to the victory?

Pray

Ask Jesus to deliver your own friends and family from the power of evil.
    Pray for the church to have a better vision of Jesus' authority.

DAY 5

Power over Sickness
Mark 1:29-34, 40-45

My mother died of cancer when I was in my teens. Her battle with the cancer was a long one and took its toll on her and the rest of our family. I will never forget the sense of powerlessness I felt in the face of her growing sickness. There was nothing I could do, nothing my father could do and, evidently, nothing that the doctors could do either.

Sickness interrupts life. It is inconvenient, time consuming and frustrating—not to mention painful. It is also unsettling because it brings with it thoughts of our limited life span. Sickness, like nothing else brings us face to face with our limits. Perhaps we spend so much money on health care in our country, not only because we want to get well, but because we are seeking to gain power over that which makes us feel so helpless.

As you read about Jesus' healings in the Gospels you will notice a sense of delighted, even exalting relief by those who are healed as well as from bystanders. In the works of Jesus a new order of reality is breaking through, something that is stronger and more overpowering than anything else known to our race.

Approach

An important element in settling in the presence of God is a sense of gratitude. When you are on intimate terms with God, there is a quiet "thank you" that frequently rises from within. Sit for several minutes in quiet, and then write down things for which you are grateful to God. (This may come as an overflow from your heart, or you may have to just do it as an exercise. Either way it's worth the effort.)

Study

1. Read Mark 1:29-34. Describe the interaction between Jesus and the mother-in-law.

2. Read Mark 1:40-45. Describe Jesus' interaction with the leper.

3. What do both healings have in common?

4. What aspects of Jesus' authority do these healings portray?

Reflect

1. If you were in the crowds and saw both healings, what would you tell your friends about Jesus?

2. In both situations, Jesus responded to a request for help. What help have you asked for from Jesus over the past couple of weeks?

What responses have you gotten?

3. The responses to Jesus' help varied. Peter's mother-in-law got up and served while the leper disobeyed Jesus' instructions to keep quiet and go to the priests. Sit back now, make a list of things you are thankful for. After you have done this, spend time expressing thanksgiving to the Lord for his powerful work in your life.

Pray

Ask Jesus to come among your family and in the church with healing power.

　　　Pray that a spirit of gratitude and obedience would characterize your family and church.

DAY 6

Jesus' Priorities
Mark 1:35-39

I am currently caught in a mode of activity that is far too busy to sustain for long. I was in my study all day, went home for forty-five minutes for dinner and then was back to church for three meetings this evening, one at 6:30, one at 7:30 and another at 8:30. Tomorrow is a full day, and then there is a meeting at 6:30 p.m. and after that a class I teach at 7:30. The following day is full as well.

There are several reasons my schedule is so packed. One is that I am new to this church, so I am learning the ropes. There is a high cost to entering any new job. Another reason for my high level of activity is that I haven't completely defined my priorities. I don't know yet what I really need to focus on to fulfill my calling here. I don't know yet what to say no to. Consequently I say yes to far too much. If I keep this pace up for long, I will suffer, my family will suffer and the church will suffer.

Jesus, thankfully, is not like me. From the very start of his ministry he knew his commission, call and priorities. In the face of ceaseless pressing demands from the crowd he was able to give freely as well as draw lines. If we too understand Jesus' priorities, we will understand him better and develop a clearer sense of what he is calling us to do.

Approach

Sometimes I am so busy that I lose any sense that the Lord is with me. Getting in touch with him means turning from my activities to the longing for personal encounter. When have you sensed that the Lord is with you recently?

How does the sense of divine fellowship correspond to your activity level?

Sit back and relax till you know that he is with you.

Study

1. Read Mark 1:35-39. After you have read today's verses, look back over the whole first chapter of Mark. Why do you think "everyone" was looking for Jesus?

2. Jesus explains his purpose to Simon and his companions. What is it?

3. How do you think Simon felt about Jesus' reply, considering that he felt a responsibility toward the people who were looking for Jesus?

4. How does Jesus view his obligation to "everyone"?

5. How do you think prayer might have affected Jesus' perspective?

Reflect

1. Examine your own interaction with the Lord. Instead of telling him how to work out his purpose for your life, spend time asking him what his purpose is. Write down how you believe the Lord is responding to you.

2. How do you think that his purposes for your life match up with your own desires and expectations?

3. Kneel before the Lord (actually or mentally), and lay before him your own desires and priorities. Look to see what he does with them and write down your impressions.

Pray

Pray for a better understanding of Jesus' mission.

DAY 7

The Spiritual Ladder of Success
Matthew 18:1-9

When we move from Mark to Matthew, we catch a rich new perspective of Jesus. While Mark wants to show us that Jesus is Lord by focusing on the *actions* of Jesus, Matthew wants us to see Jesus as Lord by focusing on his *teaching*. Matthew records the most complete account of the Sermon on the Mount (chapters 5-7), includes a couple of different sections on parables (chapters 13 and 25), and has an extensive section of teaching (chapters 18, 19 and 20) on how believers should conduct themselves in the church, his community of faith.

Whereas Mark was written to help Gentile Christian converts see the mystery of Jesus' divine nature by means of actions, Matthew was written to help Jewish converts see Jesus as the divine Lawgiver after the pattern of Moses and the Divine Son of David, the true king of Israel.

The question that Matthew addresses in this portion of his Gospel is, How can one excel in the kingdom? It's a legitimate question, how to be successful, one that we ask all the time. Jesus' answer is different from the one that the disciples expected and radically different from the one we expect today.

Approach
Good students are anxious to learn and open to receive. Distracted, preoccupied students often miss out. Prepare to receive what Jesus will teach you today by turning over your anxieties to him. Become quiet, sit for five minutes or more. Write down what comes to mind and give it up to God to take care of.

Study
1. Read Matthew 18:1-9. Write out the question posed to Jesus by the disciples in your own words.

2. We all want to be outstanding in some way. What is the difference between being great and being great*est*?

3. How does Jesus' answer address the disciples' improper motives and their desire for greatness?

4. Summarize Jesus' view of sin.

Reflect
1. In what ways do you desire not only to be good, but to better than someone else?

How do such motivations affect you and the way you relate to your competition?

2. Although the disciples didn't quite get it right, it is commendable that they wanted to do well in the kingdom of heaven. Examine your own motivations concerning the kingdom of heaven and the kingdom of this world. How do your priorities fit with Jesus' teaching?

3. Jesus is hard on sin in this passage. Ask the Lord to show you the presence of sin in your life. Write down what comes to mind.

Now take your list and mentally hand it to him. After you do, write down what you imagine that he does with it. (This little spiritual exercise is a great help for people. The spiritual interaction between the heart and Jesus is amazing.)

Pray
Ask God to create a stronger desire to become great in the kingdom within you.

Pray that a hatred of sin and pride would characterize your church.

DAY 8

The Love of the Father
Matthew 18:10-14

*A*sk a classroom of elementary children a question and watch the hands go up. Excited hands wave in the air, and boys and girls shout to get the teacher's attention, "Teacher, I know, ask me!"

Of course, when you get to high school, the response is radically different. The teacher asks a question, and there is slow-to-no response. Hands go up reluctantly if at all. It's not that the students aren't interested in attention, it's just that they are interested in attention coming from another direction, their peers. In their case, showing too much interest in the opinion of the teacher or too much knowledge could cost them the attention of their friends.

We all need attention from those we esteem, no matter who we are, how old we get or our station in life. Once we are out in the marketplace it's the attention of the supervisors and bosses that we seek. Whether they notice us and what they think of us has serious implications for the level of our income and our professional development, not to mention job security.

There is attention from another that is infinitely more important than any other, our heavenly Father. To have his gracious attention means eternal life, rivers of blessing and unending love. What a shame that his children have his undivided attention and yet aren't aware of it. In almost any church, you can find believers who compete with each other, put each other down and squabble in pursuit of what is already theirs. Those who dare to follow Jesus occupy the place of highest honor as the apple of God's eye. It only remains for us to believe it.

Approach

What do you want God to notice about you? about your efforts? your accomplishments? your hurts? Write out a few of these concerns and then sit quietly until you have a settled sense that God is paying attention to you.

Study

1. Read Matthew 18:10-14. These verses continue the discussion about the status of children and the role of humility in the kingdom of God. Jesus warns the disciples not to consider children less valuable. Explain.

2. How does the concern of the shepherd for each individual sheep expand on Jesus' teaching about humility and status in the kingdom?

3. In your own words describe the character of the heavenly Father.

4. Verse 12 begins by Jesus asking a question, "What do you think?" How would this teaching affect the disciples in their competition to be the greatest?

Reflect

1. In your mind imagine that you are surrounded by angels who are sent to protect you. Write down your responses to their presence.

2. The love of God is a pursuing love. How have you experienced his seeking you out and drawing you to himself when you were drifting away?

3. Considering the special attention that the Father gives you, how does it affect the way that you think about other believers with whom you might feel tempted to compete?

Prayer

Ask for the strength of faith to think highly of others.

   Pray for the blessing of those with whom you feel a need to compete.

DAY 9
Christian Confrontation
Matthew 18:15-20

*O*nce we know about the love of God for us, we need to be instructed on how to get along with one another. So now Matthew records for us step number two in Christian fellowship—confrontation.

Confrontation?

Does this seem surprising? Jesus knows that Christians will sin against each other. He is perfect, but he is no idealist. You probably expected Jesus to advocate forgiveness next. But before forgiveness comes confrontation. Jesus is not into cheap grace.

I am uncomfortable with this. Telling another person they have sinned against me seems judgmental, self-righteous or, well, somehow out of place. I would much prefer to pretend that it wasn't so bad after all. Of course, I will do what I can to avoid the person in the future, but I will continue to tell myself that I was not really offended in the first place. And further, if I did happen to be offended, then I will tell myself that I shouldn't be so thin-skinned.

Such thinking plays into the hands of the Evil One who loves to see walls built up between believers inside the church. When he is through, we attend church functions with skins so thick that God's love can't get through, and fellowship is merely a pretense for polite superficial chatter.

We do well to pay attention to Jesus at this point, because he charts a daring, but clarifying, way for his disciples to live together in the church.

Approach
One of the things I remember about riding in the car as a boy was the freedom to look out the window. I didn't have to know how to get anywhere, that was in Dad's hands. In a similar way, God is in control of your life. Get out of the driver's seat and trust that he knows where he is taking you. Sit back on the passenger side and relax until you know that you are not in control and feel no urge to grab the wheel. Make a note of your emotional responses.

Study
1. Read Matthew 18:15-20. List each of the steps that Jesus mentions for dealing with personal offenses in the church.

2. What is the role of fellow Christians in settling the conflict that comes from personal sin?

3. What is the role of prayer in dealing with personal conflict (vv. 19-20)?

4. What right does the church have for choosing to put unrepentant people out of the church (vv. 18-20)?

Reflect
1. Not many people follow these directions of Jesus for dealing with sin against each other in the church. Why not?

2. When have you experienced a conflict in which you were sinned against?

How did you respond?

3. Jesus promises his personal presence to deal with sinful conflicts if several believers approach him. As a first step toward dealing with a relational problem, lay it before him and ask him what he has to say about it. Then write down ideas that come to mind.

Pray
Pray for those who have offended you. Ask God's blessing on them.
   Ask God if there is something specific that he wants you to do to make peace.

DAY 10
Christian Forgiveness
Matthew 18:21-35

*P*eople were tense. The committee, more a ministry team than a decision-making group, met every September for spiritual refreshment and fellowship. In years past this group had been fun. This year, however, people were cordial, but not open.

I knew we were in trouble Friday night when the mixer games produced clinched-jawed competition rather than relaxation. My talks Friday night and Saturday morning were received with merely polite attention. A couple of people didn't come to lunch, and the rest of us felt underlying tensions rising up from beneath carefully crafted smiles. After lunch I scrapped the afternoon talk, and said, "Let's talk."

Initially, it was bleak. Hurts received and suppressed for the past year were aired. However, after problems were on the table we were able to take the next step in Christian fellowship, forgiveness. The air cleared, and the smiles were spontaneous. I was thankful for the spiritual maturity of a group in which members were free to let go of their hurts.

While there was healing, this is not a "they lived happily ever after" story. Several people left before we all faced up to our hurts. Consequently, there is still tension in committee meetings with those who have yet to experience both conflict and forgiveness. This means that we still have a ways to go before we can move on in fellowship and ministry. It is even possible that we will never get our differences completely worked out. But this too is part of being the church of Jesus Christ.

Approach

We are seldom aware of all the feelings that we experience. Like a long piece of string shoved into a drawer, our emotions become tangled and knotted. This is a problem for our sensitivity to other people and God. Sit back in quiet and give your overlooked feelings time to surface. Write them down. If you sit long enough, you will find a desire for God that you didn't even know was there.

Study

1. Read Matthew 18:21-35. Peter wants to know the limits of forgiveness. Jesus responds to Peter's question with a parable. Make a list of the characters in the parable and give a brief description of each one.

2. In this parable, what does the king find forgivable and what does he find unforgivable?

3. What is the relationship between being forgiven and forgiving others?

4. Jesus' reply to Peter's question does not directly address the number of times that Christians should forgive. From your study of this parable, why not?

Reflect
1. Make a list of as many hurts and grievances you have received from others as you can recall.

2. Evaluate your normal response to others who hurt you. How do you generally respond?

3. The heart of the wicked servant was not affected by the mercy that the king extended to him. Imagine that you are standing before the Lord. Write down what you think he has to say about your ability to forgive.

4. Our ability to forgive is based upon the gratitude for God's forgiveness of us. Spend time now thanking the Lord for his grace. Write out your prayers of thanksgiving.

Pray
Continue to pray for others who have hurt you. We need to do this frequently because it is such an important part of the Christian life.

DAY 11
Christian Faithfulness
Matthew 19:1-12

*P*assing through the town where we used to live, I called a friend to say hello. I was not prepared for the news that three of the couples in the core leadership of our previous church had divorced. What was unsettling was that these were sincere people who took God and the Scriptures seriously.

Staying married is not easy. Divorce both inside and outside the church is widespread—almost 50 percent of marriages end in divorce. One reason for this epidemic is the attitude of our culture that allows us to make commitments of convenience. Looking out for Number One and the pursuit of self-satisfaction does not encourage an environment of sticking it out in a relationship when the going gets rough.

However, as you will discover in today's quiet time, it has always been difficult to stay married. Jesus' teaching on marriage and divorce was just as radical to those who heard it as it is for us today.

Approach
Frequently, before we can get settled inwardly, we have to go through emotional turbulence. Like breaking the sound barrier, just before the

plane gets on the other side there is a great deal of vibration. Spend enough time sitting until you get past the inner turbulence to be inwardly quiet. Make notes about how you move through turbulence to quiet.

Study

1. Read Matthew 19:1-12. The Pharisees seek to involve Jesus in a controversy about divorce. Some teachers limited divorce. Others said it was permissible merely at the whim of the male, sort of an "any-fault" divorce clause. Describe how Jesus deals with their questions.

2. Jesus' limitation of divorce to "marital unfaithfulness" and the consequences of divorce for the wrong reason were stunning to the disciples and Pharisees alike (v. 10). What does that indicate about the general attitude of the people at that time toward divorce?

3. The questions about marriage, divorce and adultery raise the issue of living single. What reasons does Jesus give for staying single (vv. 11 and 12)?

4. According to these verses, what does a relationship with God have to do with living singly or lifelong marriage?

Reflect

1. Our attitude to marriage and divorce is shaped by our family and friends. What is the attitude toward lifelong marriage in your family?

What is the attitude of your friends?

2. How have you been affected by the divorce of family or friends?

3. Jesus' teaching, "The one who can accept this should accept it" could be rephrased, "Your desires reflect your calling." Look into your heart. Express on paper what your desire to be married or to be single is like.

4. Both singleness and marriage are a call and a gift from God. Thank God for whatever state you are in now. Ask God to show you some of the good consequences that come your way because of his calling. Write down what he allows you to perceive.

Pray

If you are married, pray that you both may be inwardly and outwardly chaste and faithful.

If you are single, pray that you too may be chaste and faithful to God's calling for your life.

DAY 12
Christian Commitment
Matthew 19:13-30

*S*ociologists used to teach that as the world continued to modernize, religion would drop away. However, during the past ten years that has been revised. The USA, the most advanced modern society, is also the most religious. Less than three percent of the population would describe themselves as atheist. Two-thirds of the baby-boom generation that previously dropped away from church during college has returned. These returnees are not sure what it means to be a Christian, but they know that they want to teach their children religious values and somehow they know that God fits somewhere into the mix of life.

Our church is filled with such people. Coming to church is a good start, I tell them, but not enough. Jesus is not interested in merely religious people who believe in God, who want to be good and who sincerely desire to fulfill their religious obligations. God wants more. God wants exclusive commitment. This teaching is met with puzzled looks and questions. "How is that really possible? What does that mean about my family, my career, my possessions?"

God addressed this issue with the Hebrews when he called them out of Egypt. The very first commandment is, "You shall have no other gods before me." The struggle of the Jewish nation was to discover what that meant for them. They didn't do well.

Likewise, ringing through Jesus' call, "Follow me," is the same expectation. It is the task of every believer in every generation to discover anew what it means.

Approach

Make a list of your current wants. Write them out and give them to God. Consider how your desires for them relate to your desires for God.

Study

1. Read Matthew 19:13-30. What do you know about the man from these verses?

2. What requirements does Jesus give to the man's question about how to gain eternal life?

3. Jesus mentions only five of the Ten Commandments. Look up Exodus

20:1-17. What is significant about the commandments that Jesus leaves out?

4. Contrast the disciples with the man. What have they done that is different from the man?

What benefits do they get?

Reflect
1. The First Commandment is, "You shall have no other gods before me." The Great Commandment is, "Love the Lord your God with all your heart and with all your soul and with all your mind." It was against the background of these truths that Jesus called the rich man to leave everything and follow. Make a list of everything in your life that might come before God.

Spend time in prayer placing your relationship with God before everything else in your life.
2. The issue Jesus addressed in his interaction with the young man was one

of priorities and commitment. Our possessions often reflect, and even determine, our priorities. How attached are you to your possessions?

Ask the Lord how you should think about all you own. Write down your insights and what you think he has to say to you.

3. Think back over your Christian life. What has it cost you to believe in the Lord?

What benefits, spiritual and physical, have you received?

Pray
Pray that Jesus would be the number-one desire of the members of your church.

DAY 13
Jesus' Mission
Luke 18:31-34

*E*ach of the Gospels has a unique focus and unique teaching to offer. Mark wanted us to see the mystery of Jesus' humanity and deity. By focusing on Jesus' actions, he moves us along to the conclusion that what Jesus did is more than merely human. Through Mark's presentation, we are called to believe by the power of Jesus' actions.

Matthew wanted us to see Jesus as the king of Israel, the Son of David and true Lawgiver, the one greater than Moses. He carefully presents Jesus' teaching so that in it we learn divine truth that brings us into the kingdom of heaven. Through Matthew's Gospel, we are called to believe by the power of Jesus' words.

We now turn to six quiet times in the Gospel of Luke. Luke wants us to see Jesus as a man with a supernatural purpose. The teaching of Jesus, as well as the miracles he performed, are placed by Luke in the context of Jesus' mission: going to the cross to rescue us from sin. Through the skillful writing of Luke we see Jesus as the Savior.

We should pay careful attention to Luke. In certain segments of the church words like *saved*, *salvation* and *savior* have been overused, misused and trivialized. However, in the skillful hands of Luke we can see afresh the depth and breadth of Jesus the Savior.

Approach
God has a purpose for this world and a purpose for you. For us to feel at home in his world we need to have a sense of personal purpose that fits into God's. Reflect on your own sense of personal purpose for life. What do you want to achieve in life?

Ask God to bring your purposes into harmony with his.

Study
1. Read Luke 18:31-34. What would you expect to happen to Jesus in Jerusalem if you just read verse 31?

2. What does Jesus expect to happen to him in Jerusalem in verses 32 and 33?

3. These coming events in Jerusalem were written about by the prophets. Read Isaiah 53:4-12. What painful things is the Messiah to experience?

What benefits come from his afflictions?

4. Why don't the disciples understand what Jesus is talking about (Luke 18:34)?

Reflect

1. Jesus and Isaiah are explicit about the pain that Jesus was to experience. Picture yourself in the crowd watching as Jesus is persecuted and crucified. What is your response?

2. The disciples didn't understand what Jesus was talking about. Following Jesus was confusing for them and can be for us as well. What have you found confusing/hard to understand?

How do these reflections affect your resolve to be a follower of Jesus?

3. Picture yourself standing before Jesus. Tell him you are willing to follow him wherever he leads. Write down what you sense he may be saying to you as well as your responses to his call.

Pray

Ask God to open your eyes to deeper spiritual understanding.

Ask God to give you faith to trust him for what you don't understand.

DAY 14
True Sight
Luke 18:35-43

*A*fter dismissing Christianity as old-fashioned, outdated and untrue, I was forced to reconsider when I met people whose lives seemed different. My question for them was, "How can I know that Jesus really was God?"

Their frustrating answer was, "Faith."

Initially, I didn't see this as any answer at all. How could I believe in Someone I couldn't see?

Despite the popular adage, seeing is not believing. Rather, it's the other way around. Copernicus was convinced that the popular conception of the earth as the center of the universe just didn't make sense of all the facts. He believed there was another explanation and so he looked a bit deeper. Columbus believed that there must be a better explanation than a flat world to account for ships that didn't fall off as they slipped below the horizon.

The faith of Columbus and Copernicus took them beyond sight, to the truth. After all, to our eyes, it does look like the sun goes around the earth. And, certainly, we do see ships disappear when they go beyond the horizon. In the same way Christian faith takes us beyond sight, to truth.

If Jesus were to stand before you now, as he did with those in the first century, what would you see? A man. Maybe his eyes would be penetrating, perhaps there would be a certain sense of gravity about him. But there would be no halo glowing around his head, nor would he be wearing a sign declaring him to be God. How would you know, then, that this man is God in a human body? The same way that believers for two thousand years have. By a choice to believe that comes from the conviction that there is more to this man than meets the eye.

Approach
Jesus Christ comes to us in a variety of ways. One is through the experiences of life. Make a list of things that you have done and been involved in for the past week. Write down how you felt about each one. Then pause and ask the question "How do I see the hand of the Lord behind these events?"

Events	Emotions	God's Hand

Study

1. Read Luke 18:35-43. Describe the crowd, the blind man and Jesus.

2. Besides shouting, what else does the blind man do to get Jesus' attention? (Consider the difference between addressing Jesus as "Jesus of Nazareth" and "Jesus, Son of David.")

3. How does Jesus address the man's physical, emotional, spiritual and social needs?

4. What effect would Jesus' saying "your faith has healed you" have on the blind man and the crowd?

Reflect

1. Imagine you are the blind man, and you hear that Jesus is passing by while you are at the back of the crowds. Write down what you hear, feel and do.

2. In the story there are several essential elements of healthy biblical prayer: the blind man's determination to be heard, his persistence, his knowledge of who Jesus really was and his willingness to express his need. Using the blind man as an example, rate your own prayer life.

	Poor	Good
Recognizing our blindness		
Determination to be heard		
Persistence		
Knowledge of Jesus		
Able to ask for help		

3. An important aspect of prayer is knowing who you are asking and knowing what you want. Write down what you would say to Jesus if he were to ask you, "What do you want me to do for you?"

Now close your eyes, trust that you have his attention, and tell him what you've written down. How do you feel him responding to you?

Pray
Pray for the needs of those who are close to you.

DAY 15
The Invitation
Luke 19:1-10

Recently, *Time* ran an article on new and deadlier bacteria that are developing resistance to antibiotics. Likewise, the *New York Times* ran a front-page article about a new strain of tuberculosis that was drug resistant. I found these articles unsettling.

I grew up in a world that seemed a great deal safer. A shot of penicillin was certain to remove the danger of life-threatening infection. And if the doctors didn't know what to do for an ailment, we were confident that they would in just a couple of years.

In reality, the world is not a safe place at all. A child of six in our church was diagnosed with leukemia. A retired couple looking forward to enjoying their nest egg was shattered when they discovered that the husband had colon cancer.

The world is not safe and never has been. As one sage put it, "No one gets out of life alive." All our efforts at security, whether they be medical, economic or political, run up against the reality of sin and death.

The bad news of life-threatening pain, when rightly faced, can take us to the life-saving embrace of Jesus the Savior. He is, after all, the one who actually did get out of life alive. For those who believe there is salvation. It is the secure knowledge of the world to come that is even now breaking into the dangerous uncertainty of the present.

Approach
Recall experiences of pain that you, your friends or your family experienced. Write down how you felt and how your life was affected. How did you sense the work of God in the midst of the pain?

Study
1. Read Luke 19:1-10. What was Zaccheaus like?

2. What can you find in common between the blind beggar and the rich Zaccheaus? (In both cases Jesus singles them out from the crowd.)

3. According to 19:10, Zaccheaus illustrates the essence of Jesus' purpose. Considering these verses, write Jesus' mission in your own words.

4. Jesus tells the good news that salvation has come to Zaccheaus's house. What does each of these Old Testament verses say about salvation?
Exodus 15:2:

2 Samuel 22:3:

Psalm 14:7:

Psalm 62:

What is similar to and different from what Jesus offered to Zaccheaus?

Reflect

1. Both Zaccheaus and the blind man make determined efforts to see Jesus. What effort have you made to have a relationship with Jesus?

2. Jesus responds to these efforts. Picture Jesus calling you by name and inviting himself into your house. What will you offer him?

3. Salvation for Zacchaeus meant forgiveness for his poor business ethics. What does salvation mean for you?

4. Both men respond to Jesus in life-changing ways. How are you responding to Jesus?

Pray

Ask that God's salvation would spread through the church and into the world.

DAY 16

Responsibilities and Resources
Luke 19:11-27

While I was in seminary, I worked as a house sitter for the Lewises. They took a month-long trip to some exotic part of the world several times a year. My job was to take care of the house, water the plants and generally look after things while they were gone. In return I received free room and board in a magnificent house in a very impressive neighborhood. It was a great place to live and to study.

However, the first trip they took was almost the end for me. I kept the house all right, but I was casual about watering the plants in the living room. By the time I got around to them, a couple were wilted or withering. Realizing my mistake, I gave them my frantic attention several times a day during the fourth week. They received not only water but fervent prayers as well. I'm glad to report that they did revive. The Lewises came back to healthy plants and a clean house, and I kept my job.

I think of my close call when I read today's passage. Jesus' salvation includes not only his death for our sins, but also, for a period of time, his physical absence. During that time of absence he has given us resources, physical and spiritual, to use for his purposes and our own spiritual growth. But he is coming back. When he returns, there will be an accounting. Our growth and our commendation will depend on how faithful we were.

Approach

Write down all the things you feel responsible for this week. After you have made the list tell the Lord that you want to do these things in the service of his kingdom. Make notations of your emotional responses as you go through this process.

Study

1. Read Luke 19:11-27. What are the positive and negative consequences of faithful service to the king?

2. How did the negative impression of the third servant affect his behavior?

3. Jesus is just about to enter Jerusalem. He is facing the last week of his earthly life and the events leading up to the crucifixion. How are these

impending events reflected in this parable?

4. Consider why Jesus told this parable. What impact do you think he wanted it to have on those who heard it?

Reflect
1. Our images and ideas of God affect our behavior. Sit for a while, and prayerfully make a list of impressions that you have of Jesus.

How do these impressions express themselves in your actions?

2. Jesus gave resources and responsibilities to his servants before he departed. What resources, spiritual, physical and social, has he given you for the service of his kingdom?

3. Close your eyes and imagine that Jesus has returned and you are standing before him. What do you think he might say to you?

Pray
Ask the Lord what he wants you to do in serving him. Ask for the strength to be faithful to your assignments.

DAY 17
The King's Coming
Luke 19:28-47

*L*uke continues to develop the concept of Jesus as Savior by showing us not only the benefits of believing, but also the consequences of not believing.

Since chapter 9, Luke has been describing Jesus' saving journey to Jerusalem. The scene he paints is that of an oriental king going to his capital to receive his throne. In the preceding studies you have just worked through, Jesus moved through Jericho. In today's passage, during what we refer to as Palm Sunday, Jesus moves through the outskirts of Jerusalem into the city center.

Humanly speaking this is the beginning of the climax. Jesus comes to the city amidst the praise of the people. As Messiah, he should have been received by the leaders, enthroned as king and worshiped as God.

But it didn't happen.

Luke records for us not only the glory of the day, the rejoicing and shouting of the people, but also Jesus' pain-filled prophetic lament. The salvation Jesus brings does not rescue those who choose to harden their hearts. Faith is a choice. It involves making up your mind. Unbelief is also a choice. It involves making up your mind as well. Both have consequences.

Approach
Faith is not a one-time choice, but a daily decision. Choose to believe that Jesus is Lord of your life today. One-by-one bring to him your family, friends and possessions. Sit for a while in quiet trust that he is Savior of every area of your life.

Study
1. Read Luke 19:28-47. Jesus' entry on a colt and the crowds' quoting of Psalm 118:26 (in v. 38) set a tone of a royal victory celebration as the conquering king returns to his capital. What must have been both satisfying and frustrating for Jesus about the whole experience?

2. In your own words describe Jesus' attitude toward his entry into Jerusalem. Consider his refusal to silence the crowds (vv. 39-40) and his lament over Jerusalem (v. 44).

3. Twice Jesus demonstrates knowledge of future events (vv. 30-34 and 40-44). What is the benefit and cost for him of knowing what the future holds?

4. Describe Jesus' cleansing of the temple from the viewpoint of one of the bystanders.

Now describe it from the perspective of one of the religious leaders.

Reflect

1. What must have been exciting and unsettling about these events for the disciples as they followed Jesus?

2. What is exciting and unsettling about your own experience of following Jesus?

3. The crowds were moved to acclamation and worship as Jesus approached Jerusalem on the donkey. Consider times in the past when you have been moved to public worship of Jesus. What was the experience like?

4. Jesus' exercise of his messianic authority upset the leaders by expelling those who were making a personal profit on the worship of God. Think of a time when Jesus, by his Spirit, called you to change your behavior. (If you can't think of a time in the past, consider how you think you might handle it when he does so in the future.) How did you respond?

Pray

Pray that the authority of Jesus will spread throughout the world.

DAY 18

The King's Authority
Luke 20:1-8

*D*uring the first few months after my conversion, I used to lay in bed at night worrying that God was going to make me be a missionary to Africa or, worst of all, become a minister!

I smile at those fears now. I am a pastor from choice. I can't think of anything else I would rather be. As for a missionary to Africa, I would count that a privilege too, if the call ever came. What I didn't see then, in the way I do now, is that God's authority doesn't oppress me, but brings satisfaction and fulfillment. But my early fears intuitively touched on the nature of a relationship with God. He has the right to say what I should do. He is the Creator and my Lord.

As Jesus went to the temple, his long journey should have been complete, his coronation should have taken place. But he was not crowned as king. The people loved to see Jesus work miracles, but the leaders weren't pleased. He acted too much like he was in charge and that could mean complications for them. They began to look for ways to deal with the threat of his presence. However, their plots are doomed. Whether we like it or not, if Jesus is Lord, then the consequences of both obedience and disobedience are eternal.

Approach
How do you feel and respond when your desires conflict with what God wants you to do?

Ask God to uncover hidden feelings, fears and reservations. Write down what comes to mind as you sit in silence for several minutes.

Study
1. Read Luke 20:1-8. Describe the scene in the temple as he is approached by the religious leaders.

2. What do you think is the motivation behind the question put to Jesus about his authority (v. 2)?

3. Why do you think Jesus refused to answer them?

4. How does Jesus' question about John the Baptist expose their hidden agenda?

Reflect

1. "Jesus is Lord" is one of the earliest Christian creeds. What right does he have to tell you how you should live?

How has this made a difference in the way that you have lived your life to this point?

2. Consider as many areas of your life as you can think of: home, family, friends, work, school, money, recreation, appearance, clothing, future plans. Which areas are you more inclined to try to keep personal control of?

How would your behavior change in these areas if you yielded to Jesus' authority?

3. Picture yourself before Jesus now. Ask him what you need to do to yield more of your life to him. Write down what you think he may be saying to you.

Pray

Pray that leaders within the church will be responsive to the authority of the Lord.

DAY 19

Jesus' Sentencing
John 19:1-16

The next six quiet times come from the Gospel of John. John is the most intimate of the Gospels. Like Matthew, John was one of the twelve disciples. In addition, along with Peter and James, John was one of the three disciples that Jesus took into his closest confidence. Commentators think that the reference to the "disciple that Jesus loved" is to John himself. That sense of personal contact and affection permeates the Gospel.

From the beginning to the end of his Gospel, John wants us to know that the events of Jesus' ministry were part of a bigger plan, a plan that began in eternity and opens the door to eternity for us. He pulls back the curtain slightly so that we can see the hand of the divine Director, working everything so that Jesus' rejection by the Jews becomes the opportunity for life for the entire world. In chapter 20 he summarizes his purpose, "These are written that you may believe that Jesus is the Christ, the Son of God, and that by believing you may have life in his name" (Jn 20:31). The intimacy, the eyewitness detail and the concern that we believe for eternal life combine in the last chapters of John to give us a powerful account of the crucifixion and resurrection of Jesus.

As you begin today hold in mind one of the most famous verses from John 3:16: "God so loved the world that he gave his one and only Son, that whoever believes in him shall not perish but have eternal life."

Approach
Imagine that you have just won a victory and achieved a goal that you have been working at for some time. Currently, there is nothing pressing, no looming responsibility tugging at you. Sit back, enjoy yourself and the presence of God. After you have enjoyed some rest with God, write down your feelings and thoughts.

Study
1. Read John 19:1-16. Power is an important issue in this passage. Look first at those who exercised power over Jesus. Who are they?

What can you discern of their motives?

2. What is Jesus' response to their power?

3. In what ways do we see the power of Jesus in this passage?

4. Pilate struggles with what to do about Jesus. Why didn't Jesus defend himself?

Reflect
1. A relationship with God is not only an issue of trust but of power. Just as Jesus was sent to the cross by the abuse of human power, we have all been affected in some way by the abuse of power. See if you can recall a couple of "power encounters" that were painful. Write down how they affected you.

2. We can find strength in seeing that Jesus' response to the abuse of power was trust in God. Consider how trust in God, after the example of Jesus, can help you face the pain of past hurts in power conflicts.

3. Sit back and imagine that you are standing before the throne of God. Tell God what fears you have about his power in your life. Consider too what blessings his power brings to you. After you have meditated on these things for a while, write down how it has affected you.

Pray
Ask God to give you a better understanding of his power.

DAY 20

Jesus' Crucifixion
John 19:16-27

From time to time there are pictures in the news magazines of starving children. I don't like to look at them. Turning the pages won't help. The pictures portray a painful reality, and quickly flipping the page won't make the hunger, suffering and death go away.

The crucifixion of Jesus is also a painful picture. In the history of the human race there has never been a more horrible event. The pictures of Nazi extermination camps from World War II, as terrible as they are, are mere shadows and ugly reflections of the most horrendous event in the cosmos, the murder of the Creator by the creature. It's worse than any horror movie you've ever seen or any Stephen King novel you've ever read. If we can do this, there is no crime that our race is not capable of.

And where is God in the midst of tragedy? Why doesn't he act with power? Why doesn't he rush in to save? The silence of God and the apparent absence of God tempt me to indignation and anger. However, if I am courageous enough to stare into the darkness of the crucifixion long and hard, I can see a shocking light. While the treacherous act of the human race at the crucifixion is the human race at its lowest, it is also the glory of God at its highest. God planned this. The cross of Jesus was the way it is supposed to be. There is a purpose in his death which comes to those who choose to see it.

Approach

God is with us in the hard times and dark times. Write down the good and the bad about your life, the painful and the pleasant. Ask God to draw back the curtain so that you can see the divine hand in your life. Sit and listen in silence for a while, and then write down your insights.

Study

1. Read John 19:16-27. John helps us understand the crucifixion by describing the people who were either involved or affected by it. Make a list of the people, noting what they were doing or saying.

2. Why do you think John bothered to record the details about the sign above Jesus' head?

3. Look at verses 23-24. How does the description of the dividing of Jesus' clothes give insight into Jesus' experience during the crucifixion?

4. Focus on verses 25-27. As others are observing or reacting to the crucifixion, what is Jesus doing?

Reflect
1. Based on your study of this passage, place yourself at the foot of the cross. What do you see, hear, feel?

2. In a culture that places such an emphasis on success, how do you feel about following the crucified Jesus?

3. A relationship for all believers is rooted in his call "Follow me." Come to Jesus as your crucified Lord. Ask him to bring out hesitations and reservations that could keep you from following no matter where it leads and whatever the cost.

Pray
Ask for the grace to follow where Jesus leads you in life.

DAY 21
Jesus' Death
John 19:28-37

*O*ne of the reasons that I left church as a teenager was because Christianity seemed so wimpy and anemic. The brand of preaching that I heard growing up went something like this: "God is so kind and nice and he wants us to be the same way. If we just love each other and try our best to get along, then everything will turn out all right." I must have heard the parable of the good Samaritan a dozen times before I was ten.

That brand of Christianity didn't prepare me for the death of a couple family members. My experience told me that life hurt, it was dangerous and hard. The picture of a God in heaven who just patted me on the back in the midst of pain and said, "There, there" wasn't for me.

There were a number of things that caused me to reconsider Christianity. One was the cross. Before the cross became the symbol of Christianity, it was the means of Roman execution. To understand this we might think of removing the cross at the front of the church and replacing it with more contemporary instruments of death, like an electric chair, a gun or a noose. The cross, the symbol of Christianity, provides a hard, clear-eyed exposé of life. It's a pain-filled world. We are fallen. We die. We kill each other. We killed our Creator.

The cross goes further than revealing the consequences of our sin. God knows what it means to die and has placed the curse of death on himself. Jesus was executed for us. When we pay attention to his death, Christianity moves beyond mere thoughts of kindness to confrontation with the powers that cause human pain and suffering. In the cross, Christianity becomes a religion worth believing in.

Approach

Imagine that you are in a movie theater with a large screen. Outside distractions are excluded by darkened lights and loud stereo speakers. On the screen is a story about you and God. Allow yourself to be drawn into the story. Write down some of the elements of the story line that you like. Also make a note of anything that surprises you.

Study

1. Read John 19:28-37. What were the last moments of Jesus' earthly life concerned with?

What does this reveal about him?

2. Consider verses 31-34. How was Jesus' death different from those who were crucified with him?

How is this significant?

3. According to John, what is the purpose of relating the events of the crucifixion?

4. What evidence is John presenting to affirm Jesus' identity as the Messiah, the Son of God?

Reflect
1. You have just read about the death of Jesus. In order to give you a sense of its reality consider your responses to the death of a relative or close friend. How did you feel?

How did it affect your thinking?

your actions?

your relationships?

2. Someone once said that dying is a solo act. Those around can merely watch and hold our hand. What thoughts have you had about death? Reflect and then write down your fears, anxieties and anticipations.

3. John relates the death of Jesus so that we may believe. Choose to see yourself kneeling before the Lord. Spend time in worship, thanking Jesus for his death and expressing to him how his death affects your resolve to trust him. Write down how you find yourself responding.

Pray
Ask God to help you grow in a daily application of the truth of the cross to your life.

DAY 22

Jesus' Burial
John 19:38-42

*F*unerals and graves are important parts of human life.

During a funeral, the living gather to say goodby to the dead. We need to commemorate the body of our friend or loved one and know that he or she is really gone. Studies show that those who skip the funeral often experience extended grief. They find it hard to believe, even though they know it, that the dead person is really gone.

We also have a need to remember the dead. We mark their graves with stones and inscriptions. At appropriate times of the year we send flowers. And, occasionally, we may visit the grave.

Several months ago, while attending a conference about eighty miles away from my childhood home, I felt a need to return to the grave of my mother. I hadn't been back in thirty years. We'd moved away right after her death. I'd never had a conscious desire to go to the gravesite before.

It took me awhile to locate the cemetery and then a little longer to locate the grave. I found it under a large oak tree, near the fence at the front of the grounds. I brought a bouquet of flowers along, sat down on the grave, and talked out loud about the years without her. I spoke of struggles and victories and of her grandchildren that she never knew. It was a cleansing time. As I got up to walk away, I discovered that I was able to accept, in deeper ways, both her life and her death.

As those who skip the funeral struggle with the reality of the death of their loved one, so Christians who gloss over the death of Jesus will struggle with the reality of his resurrection. As John shows us, Jesus Christ died and was buried. They embalmed him and put him in a grave.

Approach

The root word for *worry* comes from the old English word for gnawing, as a wolf gnawing at the neck of its victim. Those who walk in abiding faith learn to give over their worries to God. Sit quietly until you have a confident sense that God is with you and has driven away those howling wolves. Write a brief prayer of gratitude.

Study

1. Read John 19:38-42. Some scholars have suggested that Jesus didn't really die on the cross, that he merely fainted and later revived in the cool tomb. How would you answer them, based on your reading of this passage?

2. Look at Jesus' encounter with Nicodemus earlier in John 3:1-16. What might this secret disciple have been thinking as he helped bury Jesus?

3. How does John 3:16 foreshadow John 19:28-42?

4. You read Isaiah 53:4-12 in Day 13. Read it again. In what specific ways was this prophecy, written 700 years prior, fulfilled in the events of Jesus' death?

Reflect

1. With the death of Jesus, the secret hopes of Joseph, Nicodemus and many others seemed to come crashing down. When have you experienced the death of your hopes?

How did you feel?

2. Joseph and Nicodemus, instead of the disciples, asked for the body. Evidently, the disciples were kept away by fear of reprisals and of grief. Use your imagination to assume the role of one of the disciples. Write out what you might be thinking and feeling.

3. Isaiah writes, "We all, like sheep, have gone astray, each of us has turned to his own way; and the LORD has laid on him the iniquity of us all." Consider your own "turning away from God." We do this passively, by becoming occupied with other things, and we do this intentionally, because we want our own will rather than God's. Ask God to bring to mind your patterns and motivations for turning away. Write down your perceptions. Next thank God for sending Jesus to taking your punishment.

Patterns and Motivations of Turning Away	**Expressions of Gratitude**

Pray
Pray for the strength to keep following and believing even in the hard times of life.

DAY 23

Jesus' Empty Tomb
John 20:1-9

*O*n the evening of December 31, 1989, we stood in front the Brandenburg Gate in Berlin, waiting to greet the New Year. We were part of a large crowd gathered to celebrate the fall of the Iron Curtain and the collapse of the bondage of communist rule. For the first time since the beginning of the Cold War the gate was open and people could move back and forth between East and West Berlin. A new year and a new political era had begun.

On that first Easter morning, those who went to the tomb found it empty. There were no celebrations because they didn't understand what it meant. The empty tomb of Jesus was a gate that opened up a new era, life on the other side of death. As Jesus rose from the dead, the door to eternity was opened for those who want to enter. C. S. Lewis writes, "At present we are on the outside of the world, the wrong side of the door. We discern the freshness and purity of morning, but they do not make us fresh and pure. We cannot mingle with the splendors we see. But all the leaves of the New Testament are rustling with the rumor that it will not always be so. Some day, God willing, we shall get in."

Approach
Imagine that God has come to meet you on the front porch of a small cabin in the woods. Invite him on to the porch with you. You both sit in a couple of rocking chairs and enjoy being together looking out on the grass and trees. After sitting for a while, write down what it is like to be in his presence.

Study
1. Read John 20:1-9. As Mary approached the tomb early in the morning, what might she have been feeling as she reflected on the crucifixion and the time she spent with Jesus over the preceding three years?

2. The disciples were not expecting Jesus to rise from the dead. What questions and feelings would be on the minds of Mary, Peter and John as they saw that the tomb was empty?

3. What details does John give that indicate that Jesus' body was not in the tomb on Sunday morning?

4. John looks in the tomb, hesitates and, then entering, concludes that Jesus has risen from the dead. How would the evidence encourage that conclusion rather than believing that someone had stolen his body?

Reflect

1. John believed in the resurrection because of the evidence of the empty tomb. What is the basis upon which you believe in Jesus and the resurrection?

What difference would it make if the body of Jesus had been found in the tomb?

2. The empty tomb means that there is life on the other side of death. Imagine that you have moved through death with Jesus to the other side of life. How does it make a difference in the way you think about your work?

your family?

your friends?

your goals?

Pray

Ask for fresh insight into the new life that God has given you.

---

[1]C. S. Lewis, *The Weight of Glory* (Grand Rapids, Mich.: Eerdmans, 1965), p. 13.

DAY 24
Jesus' Appearance
John 20:10-18

I never actually expected to meet Jesus. However, the night that I became a Christian I had a personal encounter with him. I was sitting on a green-slatted pew in a little Christian camp in central Florida. (I still remember how uncomfortable it was.) I was at the meeting because of a growing spiritual curiosity and the invitation of my stepbrother. While the speaker, a successful businessman, was describing his own relationship with God, my mind began to drift toward a decision. As I was pondering whether or not to become a believer, I heard a voice. At least I was addressed in what seemed like words. What I heard was, "Steve, if you accept me, you must give up your rock group."

I was stunned. I was penetrated to the core of my being. As a teenager and aspiring flower child of the sixties, the music group was my life. My first response was no. That was asking too much. But God was persistent, and before the night was out I had surrendered.

I want to be careful here. Not everyone who becomes a Christian hears a voice. Yet, if Jesus really has risen from the dead, why shouldn't numbers of people have personal encounters with him, just as the early disciples did? I find it striking that a Gallup survey indicated that over the past decade almost a third of the American people have reported a "religious experience" or a moment of religious insight or awakening that changed the direction of their lives.

Such encounters with Jesus happen all the time, but because of our cultural bias against the spiritual side of life we don't recognize them. As Christians, we believe that through the Word of God written, preached and read, that God does in fact meet us. And in meeting us there, we can be equipped to recognize him in the whole of life's experiences.

Approach

Expectation is an important part of spiritual vitality. Imagine that you are in a room with a closed door. At any moment you are expecting the Lord to open the door, walk in and sit down with you. Write down how your expectation affects your thoughts, perspectives and attitudes about your activities and responsibilities for today.

Study

1. Read John 20:10-18. What emotions do you think Mary experienced through the course of her conversation with Jesus?

2. How is Mary's faith affected by her surroundings?

3. Why do you think hearing her name mentioned would allow her to recognize Jesus?

4. In your own words, what is the message Jesus sends to his disciples through Mary?

Reflect

1. Like Mary, our perception of Jesus is affected by our surroundings. If Jesus were to meet you in your day-to-day activities, what sort of person might you mistake him for?

2. Imagine that you have an encounter with someone who claims to be Jesus. What intimate thing might Jesus say or do that would allow you to recognize him as your Lord?

3. Because he is resurrected and alive, the Lord Jesus actually does meet us and speak to us in a wonderful variety of ways; through his written Word, through sermons, through friends and experiences of life, to mention just a few. What are some of the ways that the Lord made himself known to you in your following of him?

Pray
Ask God to give you spiritual eyes and ears to be more discerning of his abiding presence with you.

PART FIVE *The Epistles: Faith in the Lord*

DAY 25
The Call to Faith
Romans 1:1-17

*I*n these final six quiet times we move from the Gospels to the
Epistles. The Epistles, the Greek word meaning *letters,* are what I
call "in the meantime" letters. They were written so that Christians
could understand how to believe and live until Jesus comes back. They
could also be called family letters. Most were written to groups of
Christians, churches. Even those letters that aren't to communities are
written to individuals who are providing leadership for churches.

Just as Mark wrote about the beginning of the Gospel with accounts
of the continuing ministry of Jesus that we too could join in, so you can
read each letter as personally addressed to you. By believing in Jesus,
you joined the Christian community that has spread out across the globe
and through the centuries. Although there are many different church
buildings and denominations, you are members of the one body of

Christ. As you read, you join with believers through the centuries who have been instructed, guided and nourished by them.

The first two quiet times in the Epistles come from the book of Romans. Romans could be subtitled, "The Gospel According to the Apostle Paul." It contains the most comprehensive and authoritative statement of Christian beliefs ever written. In the opening verses you will see just how much the Epistles build on the Gospels. You will also discover that the sense of call and mission that the first disciples received continues even in believers who, like Paul, never met Jesus on the other side of his resurrection.

Approach
See if you can recall everything that you did yesterday, from the time you got up until you went to bed. After you are done, try to recall the variety of emotions that you experienced throughout the day. Once you have listed your events and emotions, give them over to God. Ask him to show you how he was with you and then write down your impressions.

Events	Emotions	God's Presence

Study

1. Read Romans 1:1-6. Paul's sense of mission and the gospel are inextricably bound together. From these verses, see if you can unravel what Paul thinks about himself and what he thinks about Jesus Christ.

2. Read 1:7-13. Paul has never been to Rome, but he is obviously eager to go. How would you summarize Paul's attitude toward the Roman Christians?

What does he hope to accomplish by going to see them?

3. Read 1:14-17. These verses are a glimpse into the character of the great apostle. Describe his sense of mission.

4. If these verses were the only portion of Scripture that you had access to, how would you define and describe the gospel? (Be as complete and detailed as you can be in your summary.)

Reflect

1. Paul writes that he is not ashamed of the gospel because it is the power of God for salvation. When have you been tempted to feel "ashamed of the gospel"?

When have you felt proud of the gospel?

2. Paul mentions the mutual encouragement that comes from sharing our faith with fellow Christians. When and where have you personally experienced such a strengthening?

3. Plan to build on this truth of faith-sharing. Who can you make plans to spend time sharing your faith with that will be mutually beneficial?

4. Not many of us are called to be apostles or missionaries like Paul. However, every Christian receives a call from the Lord to believe and obey. Ask the Lord to show or affirm his call to you and for your life. Write down what you sense he is saying.

Pray
Ask God what mission he has for you. Pray that all God's people would be proud, rather than ashamed, of the gospel.

DAY 26
The Gift of Righteousness
Romans 3:19-26

*I*n *The Closing of the American Mind,* Alan Bloom writes that the only sin left in America is to say that there is sin. We live in a culture that has given up its morality. We now talk about values when we want to talk about human behavior. However, the word *value* addresses our behavior as merely personal preferences, not as right or wrong. Suggest that someone might be doing something wrong and eyebrows are raised. People start muttering about the need to keep an open mind and how important it is not to be judgmental. The term to describe this way of thinking about human behavior is *relativism.*

Because of relativism, it is difficult to understand one of the central truths of the Bible—righteousness. From Genesis to Revelation, the Scriptures record that God is righteous. We can begin to understand what this means by saying that he is trustworthy, just, good and hates evil. Human beings made in his image are to be righteous as well. This includes the idea that our thoughts and actions are moral. They can be right and they can be wrong. They can be good and they can be bad.

When Adam and Eve chose to disobey God their actions were morally wrong—unrighteous. The consequence of their act created a moral deformity in our race, and all their children inherited the birth defect of unrighteousness. It was for this purpose, to address the condition of unrighteousness that Jesus Christ became human and died on the cross.

Approach
An image that David used to describe God is that of the shepherd. In Psalm 23 he wrote that God leads him beside still waters. In order to settle today let's use that image. See yourself being led to green pastures and a clear cool pond. Sit down for a while in the presence of the Lord and enjoy his affection and protection. After sitting for a while, write down what difference your time with him makes in the way that you look at the issues and tasks that you face.

Study
1. Read Romans 3:19-26. What words and phrases are used to describe the universal problem of sin?

2. Why isn't personal effort in keeping the Law sufficient to keep us in a good relationship with God?

3. How is Jesus Christ the universal solution? (Paul's line of argument may be a bit hard to follow, but it's worth paying close attention to.)

4. Paul began in chapter 1 by describing the gospel as the gospel of God. Notice every time the word *God* is used, and write down all that he has done for us.

Reflect
1. Sin results in keeping God at a spiritual and emotional distance. Reflect on the presence and the effects of sin in your life. What are your perceptions?

2. Righteousness means that we can be in a living relationship with God. It comes as a free gift to those who believe in Jesus. See yourself standing before God. Tell him you believe in Jesus. How do you respond as he gives to you the gift of righteousness?

3. Gratitude is the proper response to the gift of righteousness. Imagine that your heart has in it a spring of gratitude that is welling up from deep inside. As it follows up and out write down how you feel.

Pray
Pray for the spread of righteousness throughout the world, overcoming sin and turning people back to God.

DAY 27
The Foolishness of the Cross
1 Corinthians 1:18-31

The cross doesn't make sense to the modern mind. Someone who sees human actions as personal preferences will think that the cross of Jesus Christ is foolish. After all, why does Jesus need to die to eradicate unrighteousness when there is no such thing as sin?

But then the cross has never made sense to the human mind. At the heart of an unrighteous race, there is a need to explain life and understand the world without reference to God. This predisposition to obscure God can create social problems for Christians. It makes us out of step with socially accepted opinion. Like people who show up at a costume party without a costume or come to a formal dinner without a coat and tie, we will frequently seem out of place.

This social pressure, unless we are prepared to face it, can create problems for Christians. We may feel so embarrassed that we never talk about our faith and even begin to think and act like we don't believe. This is a tragedy because it leads to the loss of the pleasure of knowing

God. The other danger is that we become so defensive that we set up walls to protect ourselves and keep out the unbelievers. This destroys our call to be missionaries functioning as salt and light in the world.

It is important that Christians understand and believe that while the cross seems foolish to the world, it takes us to the very core of life's meaning.

Approach
Our hearts can become like cluttered closets. Open the door of your heart to God. Ask him to clean it up and organize it. As you allow God to do his work, pay attention to what he does and how you respond. Write down your impressions.

Study
1. Read 1 Corinthians 1:18-31. The call of God comes up again (vv. 26-31). What does Paul want the people of Corinth to know about their call?

2. Paul contrasts the way of the world and the way of God using the concepts of wisdom and foolishness. Compare the wisdom and foolishness of the world with the wisdom and foolishness of God.

The Wisdom and Foolishness of the World	The Wisdom and Foolishness of God

3. How is the cross the essence of the wisdom and foolishness of God?

4. Paul says that Jesus is our wisdom from God—that is, our righteousness, holiness and redemption. Look up each word in a Bible dictionary. How would you define each of these terms?
Wisdom:

Righteousness:

Holiness:

Redemption:

Reflect
1. The gospel appeared to be foolish to most of those to whom Paul preached. What is the prevailing attitude toward Jesus in our culture? As you reflect on this consider some of the different aspects of your life. Our culture in general:

Your work:

Your family of origin:

Your schooling:

Your friends:

2. How do people in the preceding areas view you as a Christian?

3. For the Christian, all of life is to be seen from the perspective of the cross. See yourself kneeling before the cross of Christ. Hold up each important area of your life before the cross, and write down what you observe. Our culture in general:

Your work:

Your family of origin:

Your schooling:

Your friends:

Pray
Ask God to give you a humble sense of confidence in the truth and wisdom of the gospel.

DAY 28

The Power of the Cross
Colossians 2:9-15

The archbishop of Canterbury, George Carey, has written a book on the cross entitled *The Gate of Glory*. What a wonderful title! Because of Jesus' death, we can get past the barrier of sin and move into an eternal intimate relationship with God. Although Carey didn't intend to imply this, many people see the cross as merely a way that they leave behind as they grow in Christ.

During one of my quiet times, I had a vision of my life with Christ that caused me to see the cross in a whole new way. Over the years I have worked hard at Christian growth and ministry. However, what I saw in that time of reflection was painful and unsettling. Mixed in with laudable desires was the use of Christ, the Scriptures and others for my own agenda. The words of Paul in Romans struck with painful force, "So I find this law at work: When I want to do good, evil is right there with me" (Rom 7:21).

From that vision I began to see that the cross was not only a *gate of glory* but the *bridge of glory* as well. The cross is the bridge between the gap of my growing knowledge of God's righteousness and the growing knowledge of my divided heart. The glorious relief comes in seeing that cross which opened the door, continues to grow in size and power in order to bridge the gap.

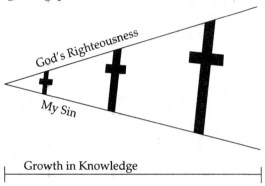

Approach
Choose to see the cross as the bridge between you and God. Observe what this vision of the cross does with your priorities and actions. Write down how it allows you to face negative feelings that you harbor concerning your past thoughts and actions.

Study
1. Read Colossians 2:9-15. Circumcision was the Old Testament sign of belonging to God. Paul explains that this Old Testament concept of the physical cutting away of human flesh is spiritually transformed by the work of Christ. After reading over these verses, in your own

words define the circumcision of Christ.

2. Paul also writes that the Old Testament Law was affected by the work of Christ. How does the cross affect these laws and regulations?

3. Jesus Christ not only rescues us from the condemnation of the Law, but from our own sinful natures as well. According to Paul, how does God work this transformation?

4. Not only does Jesus Christ rescue us from the Law, and our own sinful natures, but he also rescues us from hostile spiritual powers. How is it that removing the condemning effects of the Law by the cross would also disarm them?

Reflect
1. Imagine that you are standing before God at the final judgment. Arrayed against you are the laws of God that you have broken and the spiritual beings who want to see you condemned. On your side, however, is Jesus who brings his work to your rescue. Allow the court scene to be played out in your mind. Describe the interaction.

What are your feelings?

2. Let's change the scene. Since the cross is the means by which our deliverance and transformation takes place, put yourself at the cross. Imagine that any law that you have broken and would bring guilt is being nailed to the cross above the head of Jesus Christ. Describe how you feel.

3. The work of Christ brings a transformation inside us. Reflect back over the past few months. How are you aware of the spiritual work of Christ to make you more godly and less sinful?

Pray
Ask God to help you live every day in the light of the cross.

DAY 29

The Resurrected Life
1 Peter 1:3-9

W hen we are born again through the work of Jesus Christ on the cross, there is a great deal of work to be done. Getting a new heart does not necessarily mean that we will get a new mind to go along with it.

We live in a culture that has chosen to be blind to the spiritual side of life for the past 200 years. It has taken a great deal of philosophical and educational effort to get us to this point where the spiritual is absent from our consciousness. We have been carefully taught that there is no such thing as the supernatural, that there are no such things as angels or demons, and that heaven is a merely a fairy tale for those who are afraid to die.

If we are to think differently then we must begin a process of reeducation. We need to learn that the spiritual is real; that angels and demons do exist and that heaven is as real as the solid ground under our feet. Without a reeducation we will live as split personalities. Our hearts will always be pulling us toward heaven, but our minds will continue to focus exclusively on the physical side of life, and we will think that only the here and now is important.

God is not willing to leave us in such a confused state of affairs. Behind the scenes he is moving and shaping the experiences of our lives so that we will not be of heavenly heart and worldly mind. Through experiences of pain and suffering, as well as times of peace and comfort, God is molding and shaping a new way of thinking. He wants to see not merely the flat dimension of physical reality, but the depth of the spiritual and the physical.

Approach
The word *confused* means that there is a fusion or a mixture of conflicting ideas and motives. The word *sincere* means to have unmixed motives. Ask God to expose the places where there is a fusion of godly and ungodly thinking in your mind. Sit quietly and let God bring some of your mixed thinking to the surface. Write down what comes to mind. After a period of time, offer your list up to God and ask him to purify your mind and make it sincere.

Study
1. Read 1 Peter 1:3-9. Describe the emotional tone of Peter in these verses.

2. This epistle gives us insight into Peter the apostle. Summarize the work of Jesus Christ according to Peter's words in these opening verses.

3. The Christian life is not easy. How should Christians think about suffering and faith?

4. According to Peter, what should be the role of heaven in the thought life of the Christian?

Reflect
1. All of us experience pain and suffering. How have these made a difference in the way you live and think about yourself, God, your work and your relationships?

2. Peter writes that painful experiences purify our faith. Imagine that you are gold ore being melted in a pot to bring out the impurities. Write down what impurities you see God bringing to the surface.

3. Imagine that you are absolutely certain that your future safety, comfort and importance are assured, that there is nothing that anyone could do to take these away from you. How would it make a difference in the way you related to your family, went about your work and used your money?

The good news is that this security is true, through your faith in Jesus

Christ. Thank God for your salvation and sit for a while resting in the safety of your position.

Pray
Ask God to give you the pure faith that allows you to trust him for your earthly and heavenly future.

Pray that his return would be soon in order to bring justice to this needy confused world.

DAY 30

The Life of Hope
Revelation 1:4-8

The drama of the world began in Genesis with the creation and the Fall. It is completed in the future with the events written about in the book of Revelation. There is much in it that is not clear. It uses prophetic pictures that are not easy to understand. However, what is clear is that there is a coming end to history as we know it, and Jesus Christ is coming back.

When you risk following Jesus Christ the future opens up to you. My final objection to Christianity melted when I was told that Jesus Christ was coming back. It finally made sense. I knew that Jesus was supposed to have risen from the dead. I was told that he had gone to heaven. But somehow that was incomplete. If Jesus fixed the world by his life and death, then why wasn't the world fixed?

The answer is that the world will be. Jesus set the kingdom of heaven in motion and is coming back to consummate it. When Jesus came the first time, by his powerful works, he showed what he was capable of.

When he returns his power will be extended to all—whether they believe in him or not.

The broader picture of Christianity is that Jesus is not merely my personal Savior—he is the Savior of the world. He is not merely my Lord—he is the Lord of the world. When he returns it will be to universal recognition and rule. The curse will be removed, the wicked will be judged, and the world will be restored to the righteous paradise it was before the Fall. God will again dwell among his people, and he will receive the worship and glory due his name.

Approach
Growing up on the west coast of Florida, I loved to watch the sun set while walking along the beach. I found there a sense of peace and personal communion with God. My goals and struggles always seemed less pressing. Where do you find that special place of refreshment? Wherever it is, think about it, and then write down your description. After you have described it, get quiet inwardly so that you can enter into the presence of God.

Study
1. Read Revelation 1:4-8. After listing the different titles used for Jesus Christ in these verses, summarize in your own words what they mean.

2. What is universal, and what is personal about the ministry of Jesus Christ?

Universal	Personal

3. There are those who suggest that Jesus' Second Coming will be secret. What would you say to them based on these verses?

4. What does it mean that God is the "Alpha and Omega" (the first and last letters in the Greek alphabet) "who is, and who was, and who is to come"?

Reflect

1. Grace and peace come us from the throne room of heaven where Jesus Christ is Lord. Look up these words and write out their definitions:

Grace:

Peace:

How have you experienced the grace and peace of Jesus Christ through your quiet times in this guide?

2. Jesus Christ is the One who has washed us in his blood. That is the biblical image of a priest who brings the forgiveness of sins by means of the sacrifice of an animal. However, Jesus is the priest who offered his own blood rather than that of an animal. Imagine your heart, covered with the grime of sin, being washed by the blood of Jesus Christ. Write down what it is like.

3. The development of these verses begins with grace coming from God (vv. 4-5a), and is followed by a response of worship (vv. 5b-6) from his people. Based on your experience of the grace of God write out as many good things as you can about why you appreciate God and are grateful to him. After you have written your praises, just sit back for a while in silent heartfelt appreciation.

Pray
Ask God to move his church to live in anticipation of Jesus' return.